LIVING SACRED CEREMONY

EARTH INSPIRED PRACTICES FOR TRANSFORMING & CELEBRATING

NATALIA KAROWAY

Copyright © 2015 Natalia Karoway
www.SweetAndSacred.com

All rights reserved. No part of this book may be reproduced by any means without written permission from the author.

Photography by Addie Roberge
www.AddieRobergePhotography.com

ISBN-13: 978-1514675342
ISBN-10: 151467534X

CONTENTS

INTRODUCTION   8

My Life in Ceremony   8
What is Ceremony?   9
Ceremony to Empower   9
Celebration in Ceremony   11
Things to Keep in Mind   11
A Note on Permission   12
Where to Begin   12

THE CEREMONIES   13

Awakening Sacred Space   15
Embodying Sacred Reciprocity   19
Water Blessing   23
Despacho Ceremony   26
Santa Tierras   30
Nourish, Transform & Heal   34
Soul Awakening   38
Deep Earth Connection   42
Sacred Endings   46
Destiny Lines   50
Growing Forgiveness   54
Moon Mama   58
Sacred Workspace   62
Making Medicine   66

Celebrating Love   70
Making Space for Money   74
Burn it Up   78
The Beauty of Gratitude   82
Returning to Now   86
Simplification   92
Calming The Storm   96
Calling in Love   100
Sacred Celebration   104
Honoring the Sun   108
Align to the Divine   110
Strengthening Family Roots   114
Fire Cleanse   118
Bringing Balance   122

CLOSING THOUGHTS   126

ACKNOWLEDGMENTS   126

ABOUT NATALIA   128

INTRODUCTION

MY LIFE IN CEREMONY

When I first stepped on to the shamanic path, I was immediately taken with the idea of ceremony. It was so foreign to me at that time (coming from a non-religious upbringing), so I approached ceremonies with wide-eyed curiosity and awe. Coming from a creative background, I fell in love with the art of the despacho* ceremony, with its attention to fine detail and the visual beauty within its creation. But more than the fascination I had with such a deeply rooted tradition, it was the result of my work in ceremony that inspired my full on love affair.

When I think of the stories I can share from the many ceremonies I have held, they almost seem unbelievable, even to me. There is power in constantly being humbled by the gifts of spirit. But the results are my truth and they are shared to inspire you to delve into ceremonial exploration for your own healing and transformation.

- Ceremony has supported my body's healing on multiple occasions. One of my most profound stories is shared within my Moon Mama ceremony.

- Ceremony has offered me spontaneous transformation—as in the intention I brought to ceremony was met instantaneously.

- Participating in ceremony has dramatically changed my relationship to money.

- Ceremony assisted in the sale of my house with the utmost ease. Learn more in the Despacho Ceremony (page 26) and Santa Tierras (page 30).

- Ceremony has helped to align me with new homes that fit exact descriptions of what I have prayed for—and quite quickly, I might add.

- Ceremony has given me information on how and when to move forward.

- Ceremony has transformed relationships.

- Most importantly, ceremony has connected me with spirit and mother earth more deeply than I ever imagined.

What possibilities exist for the way ceremony can transform your life? In my eyes, every possibility imaginable!

*A despacho is a traditional Andean earth offering that you will learn more about on page 26

WHAT IS CEREMONY?

The way I approach ceremony through this guide is:

> ### CEREMONY
> *Stepping outside of the mundane world to commune with spirit in a deeply sacred way. This transcendent encounter includes crystal clear intention, heartfelt prayer, offerings of reciprocity and visual beauty.*

The best way to understand ceremony, like anything in life, is to participate. Experience the ceremonies along this journey and create your own methods as you feel inspired to evolve the above definition to fit your life.

However ceremony lives within you, keep on fanning its flames! Share it with others, teach your children, honor your friends, and bring it to your place of work. Ceremony heals and transforms in a way that is so needed on our planet at this time. It is our duty to carry this medicine forward.

CEREMONY TO EMPOWER

As much as I adore working one-on-one with clients to shift, shed, and heal from the messiness of life, it is far more important to me that I can empower you to do your own healing work when appropriate. Even when I share shamanic healing with a client, I always recommend following sessions with a personal ceremony that puts the power of healing back in the individual's own hands.

In my own life, I have had plenty of opportunities to work with amazing shamans for healing and transformation. When I felt that the majority of my work had been completed at the hands of others, I embraced ceremonies that allowed me to work with my own energy when healing was needed. When challenges emerged, these practices became my number one tool for self-healing and they still remain there today. Ceremony is also my path to prayer, manifestation, and celebration.

The beauty of ceremony is that its power is accessible to all—as long as you are at least open to the possibility that ceremony can shift things. You don't have to know how or why, but your open heart and open mind are always the keys.

CELEBRATION IN CEREMONY

In my line of work, it can seem like I am always deep in the trenches of trauma and drama. Another reason I love ceremony so deeply is that it is not just for healing and fixing things. Ceremony is for celebrating the beauty of life in a way that we become aligned with attracting more and more of this goodness.

Ceremony focuses on gratitude for the blessings we have and prayer for more blessings to come. I adore this aspect of ceremony where we remember that nothing should be taken for granted. I almost look at it as shamanic preventative medicine. It keeps me energetically aligned, focused on my intentions, and clear in my actions. I truly believe that regularly engaging in ceremony can keep you on your highest path.

THINGS TO KEEP IN MIND

Every ceremony that you create will be uniquely beautiful. However, there are some aspects that will remain a common thread in all ceremonies.

- Always create a sacred space for your ceremonies. You will learn to do this in Awakening Sacred Space (page 15).

- Always bring a gift for spirit. We never take without first making an offering of ourselves. You will practice this within Embodying Sacred Reciprocity (page 19).

- Enter your ceremonial space with a clear mind and an open, loving heart. If you're angry, distracted or otherwise feeling a little less than your vibrant self, perhaps choose another moment to engage in this sacred work. Anything that is going to keep you from staying clear with your intention of healing, transforming, or celebrating needs to be checked at the door.

- The main ingredient in every single ceremony is solid intention. Getting really clear about what you are looking to create and the energy you wish to bring to the ceremony is critical. I make sure to clear my thoughts and focus my intent before I even set up my sacred space. Is the ceremony to heal? To release? To transform? To forgive? The most clear and refined intention will set the stage for the entire ceremony.

- Always use natural and biodegradable ingredients for your offerings. These ceremonies include gifts for the earth and spirit. The last thing we want to leave behind is man made waste. Going out to gather natural materials from your local environment can be part of the ceremony itself.

- Bring no expectations. As I mentioned previously, I am constantly humbled and surprised by the miraculous results of ceremony. This childlike excitement is only accessible to me because I don't expect a certain outcome. I align myself to receive the blessings of spirit but I don't predict or expect them to come in a certain package. The lack of attachment to an exact result allows for the magic to happen.

- Don't take shortcuts. Laziness has no place in ceremony. It is my belief that the deliberate, methodical, and intentional actions within a ceremony show spirit that we mean business. This devotion is mirrored back to us with impeccable results.

- Try to step out the way. This is a bit of a dance. We want to focus on our intention for sitting in ceremony at this particular time. Yet, we really want spirit to run the show and to guide our actions. Stay in a state of prayer, light in your thoughts, and over time you will find the practice of ceremony to become more co-creative with spirit.

- Watch for opportunities post-ceremony. I love this part. Be aware of the sometimes subtle magic that unfolds in the days and weeks following your work. You don't want to get so distracted in life that you miss just how beautiful the gifts from spirit can be.

A NOTE ON PERMISSION

In the practice of shamanism, we always work with permission when praying on behalf of others. If you plan to hold ceremony in honor of another person's healing, make absolute certain that you clearly have permission for the exact intention you are bringing. It is completely unethical to assume that we know what another person truly wants in life, no matter how clear you think it may be. Please don't hold this lightly or make your own rules here. If you are unable to ask permission because of the state another person may be in (for example, in the case of serious illness or accidents) the intention behind your ceremony may be that this person's soul is fulfilled in whatever way this individual truly desires.

WHERE TO BEGIN

I recommend beginning with Awakening Sacred Space (page 15) followed by Embodying Sacred Reciprocity (page 19). These ceremonies are the foundation for every other ceremony along this journey. After that, skim through and find the ceremony that best aligns with your needs at this time and dive right in.

THE CEREMONIES

AWAKENING SACRED SPACE

Sacred space does not need to be limited to the confines of certain locations. No matter where we are in any moment, we can create a sacred setting to do our healing and ceremonial work. The intention is to make a shift from ordinary reality into the extraordinary where magic and miracles can unfold, while also requesting the presence of spirit for support.

All of the ceremonies that you create from this point forward should begin by awakening sacred space. This practice will become your own, so I encourage you to find joy in creating your unique ceremony. I will give you a beautiful but basic foundation and the rest is up to you.

If the space you choose to do your healing work has any funky energy, the first time you do this sacred space practice, have your intention be to clear the space. You can do that very quickly and effectively with this method.

MATERIALS

- Candles
- Scent of choice
- Drum, rattle or music
- Crystals, herbs, etc. and anything else that invokes the sacred for you

THE CEREMONY

1. Set your intention for the work you will be doing today. Why are you summoning spirit? Speak your intention aloud as your opening prayer. For example:

> *"Mother Earth, Father Sun, Grandmother Moon, Great Spirit. I ask for your presence and blessing as I sit in ceremony today. Please clear this space of any heavy or stagnant energy. Please fill it with the energy of unconditional love and healing. Please sit with me and work through me. Please accept my offerings and my gratitude for your assistance."*

2. Light a candle.
3. Bring in a scent to awaken your perception and clear the space. Fragrance is also an offering to spirit. Light sage or palo santo, diffuse some essential oils, mist some rose water—whatever you love!

4. Bang a drum, shake a rattle, ring a bell or put on some sacred music while calling out to your spirit guides, the spirit of your land, pachamama, goddesses, ascended masters, guardian angels—whoever you define as spirit. Ask them to join you in your space and to support your healing & ceremonial work. Call until you feel a shift in the air, in yourself, in the energy—they have come! Do not worry if you're not feeling something profound your first few times. Sensing the shift is a skill you can and will develop over time with commitment to sacred work.

5. Your sacred space is now set!

6. Once a ceremony is complete, remember to thank and release spirit in a vocal prayer as you blow out your candles and quiet your music.

NOTES FOR YOUR OWN CEREMONY

EMBODYING SACRED RECIPROCITY

> ***Ayni*** - *Giving & receiving equally. Sacred reciprocity. Right relationship with both the physical and spiritual world. Balance & harmony.*

The heart of most ceremonies is about returning to ayni. When we give, we receive and we give again... the cycle continues infinitely. But when we take too much, we are weighed down. And when we give too much, we are left hungry.

A simple way to return to the rhythm of ayni is by making simple offerings to pachamama— the spirit of our mother earth. When we pick a flower, when we have a beautiful walk in the forest, when we enjoy an abundant meal, we give back to her for providing this joy and nourishment. This will be an imperative practice along your ceremonial and spiritual path.

To begin and stay in the practice, you will fill a medicine bag with sacred offerings and keep it close so you can always be prepared to give.

MATERIALS

- A small pouch
- Dried herbs or flowers

THE CEREMONY

1. Awaken sacred space
2. Gather herbs or dried flowers that are sacred to the land that you walk on. Different parts of the world are going to have plants that are uniquely sacred to the local land. Find out what those plants are for you!
3. Don't know where to begin? My bag has tobacco, sage, lavender and rose petals. In the Andes, the gift is always coca leaves. Find a blend that is your signature as you begin to cultivate this deeper relationship with spirit.
4. Start to create a practice of sprinkling a pinch of your special blend onto the earth anytime you are out having an experience in nature. You can also begin a daily practice, as I have, to leave an offering with a prayer of gratitude for all of the beauty and blessings in life.

5. Infuse your offering with the highest intention of gratitude for all that you have and for all that the earth has given. In this tradition, we use our breath to charge the offerings with the energies of our prayers. Say your prayer, breathe onto your offerings and sprinkle them onto the earth.

> *Each time you engage in this practice, you are helping to grow the roots of stronger and stronger ayni. When your life is truly in ayni, synchronicity seems commonplace and your days flow with ease. You will soon find this practice is well worth the simple effort.*

NOTES FOR YOUR OWN CEREMONY

WATER BLESSING

Though it does not seem possible, as a collective, we have forgotten the value of our earth's precious waters. We have polluted, wasted and taken for granted the very liquid that nourishes our lives. Water blessings are a way to let the spirit of water know that some of us remember and that we also choose to remind others, as we collectively awaken. These ceremonies can be as simple as praying and expressing gratitude to the water we use for drinking, bathing, cooking, gardening, and cleaning. Or, they can be more elaborate and intentional like this Peruvian inspired water despacho or offering.

A shaman's power to heal and transform is based on relationships with spiritual allies. If you are looking to create a powerful relationship with a body of water, this is a wonderful ceremony to plant the seeds of that alliance.

This offering is truly an unconditional expression of gratitude. I don't include personal prayers or requests in this type of despacho. If you are looking for your own healing or transformation, you may wish to create a traditional despacho instead (page 26).

This offering is best made by the water's edge so you can place it right in once complete. Be aware of winds and the flow of the water, choosing a place where the water will take the offering rather than push it back to shore.

MATERIALS

- 1 large, round loaf of bread
- 2-4 dozen carnations, depending on the size of your bread
- A few large handfuls of whole bay leaves, in good condition
- Lots of candies - In Peru, the shamans love to offer sweets & chocolates to spirit
- A glass of red wine
- A small stick

THE CEREMONY

1. Awaken sacred space, making sure to invite the spirit of the water you are blessing with strong intention.

2. If you are creating this ceremony as a group, everyone will participate, but it is helpful to have one or two people build the offering, holding the pure, undistracted intention of gratitude and honoring. It is also fine and very sweet to do this ceremony on your own.

3. Begin to distribute your materials among participants. Everyone should have a carnation or a few depending on how many people are present. Participants should also have a kintu or two of bay leaves. In the Andean tradition, we make kintus, a bundle of 3 coca leaves, to hold our prayers. In parts of the world where we do not have access to coca leaves, we use bay leaves and call on the spirit of mama coca to infuse them. You are welcome to use any leaves that inspire you.

4. Sit quietly with your intentions of gratitude for the spirit of water. Use each flower and kintu as a prayer catcher, infusing them with your breath. Each intentional breath carries the spirit of your blessings.

5. Collect the flowers and kintus as you begin to assemble your despacho. Lay out your bread and use the stick to poke holes where the flowers will sit.

6. Make a ring of flowers around the outer edge of the bread. Then, make a cross of flowers in the center.

7. Add the kintus, surrounding the flowers, and fitting them in as desired.

8. As the ceremony leader, you will infuse the candies with prayers and blessings of gratitude through your breath. Once they are ready, fill the four chambers created by the cross of flowers and sprinkle them around the entire despacho as you wish.

9. Use a carnation, dipped in red wine, to sprinkle a final blessing over the despacho. Pass the wine so everyone has a chance for this last blessing.

10. When the despacho feels complete, bring it to the water's edge and say a final prayer, asking the spirit of this water to accept your offering of gratitude. If necessary, carry it into the water a little ways so it won't float back to shore. Gently place the offering so it floats away for the spirit of water to consume!

11. Close your sacred space and enjoy the beauty that surrounds you as long as you wish!

NOTES FOR YOUR OWN CEREMONY

DESPACHO CEREMONY

In the Andes of Peru, the creation of despachos, or offering bundles, are the essential sacred ceremony. Despachos are created regularly as offerings to pachamama (mother earth) and the apus (high mountain spirits). The Peruvian paqos, or shamans, create their offerings with absolute beauty, reverence, and intention.

The bundles are made up of many ingredients, each having its own significance. In Peru, you will see kintus (bundles of 3 coca leaves), candies, flowers, cookies, figurines, play money, confetti, cotton, string, llama fat, glitter, shells, gold foil, seeds, corn, rice, sugar, spices, wine, and more. These ingredients are a combination of gifts for pachamama and symbols for our own health, happiness, abundance, and fulfillment. Every paco that I have experienced adds his or her own personal signature to the despacho even if the ingredients are the same.

Prayers are infused into each individual object through the breath as they are artfully and intentionally added to the despacho. Together, the ingredients create a beautiful mandala. Once complete, the bundle is wrapped up and either burned, buried in the earth, or released in running water.

We can bring our own personal prayers to a despacho as an exchange with spirit. When we ask for help, we are willing to give in return. This keeps us in ayni—the practice of sacred reciprocity and ultimate balance.

Despacho ceremonies are extremely transformative and beneficial in my life. I choose not to work with rules in my own creation process. Rather, I use ingredients that I have available, that are biodegradable and that resonate with me for the particular despacho I am creating. And of course, my main ingredient is rock solid intention.

When my husband and I were ready to sell our home, we created a beautiful and deeply intentional despacho to bury on our land. We received the perfect offer in just 3 days after listing the house on the market. I completely trust that this energetic exchange between us and pachamama worked magic on bringing the sale to life!

I will share very loose and basic outlines so you can add your own personal touch to the ceremony and begin to create your signature despacho. This is another great way to build relationships with spirit. When they smell your particular despacho being burned, they know it is your soul calling for support! As with everything in Living Sacred Ceremony, your benefits will be as strong as your intention.

MATERIALS

- Large white sheet of paper
- Flowers
- Handfuls of whole bay leaves, in good condition, for kintus
- Biodegradable objects that resonate with you: seeds, herbs, plants, foods, sugar, etc.
- Any other biodegradable objects that symbolize your specific prayers
- Plants or herbs with scents that are sacred to your location
- Cotton string to tie the bundle
- Materials for a fire if you choose to burn the despacho

THE CEREMONY

1. Awaken sacred space.
2. Lay your paper on the ground.
3. Begin to create your mandala. Infuse each object that you place on the paper with your breath and prayer. I like all objects, except for my kintus, to hold prayers of unconditional love and gratitude to pachamama. I save the kintus for my personal prayers.
4. Gather your kintus, using one bundle of 3 bay leaves for each personal prayer. Take some deeply focused time to pray and infuse the kintus with your prayer, intention, and breath.
5. Add the kintus to your mandala and sense if there is anything else you would like to add to complete your despacho.

> *Despachos are the ceremony that I turn to the most. They are beautiful, powerful, and transformational. I absolutely love sharing them in community and seeing our individual prayers come together as one vibrant offering.*

6. When you feel complete, wrap the paper around the objects like a gift—it is one, after all! Tie it closed with the string so nothing falls out.

7. I prefer to burn despachos in a fire pit. It is believed that this will bring about the quickest results. When burning, it is not considered polite to watch the despacho. You can check in occasionally just to make sure it burns completely. If burning is not an option, bury the despacho in the earth or let the ingredients float away in running water, such as a stream or river. This is why it is important to use natural objects.

8. Close sacred space once your offering has been made. As your prayers begin to be answered, remember to continuously give gratitude and offerings to spirit. We don't want to use these ceremonies only when something is out of balance. Rather, think of using them to maintain the goodness of life.

NOTES FOR YOUR OWN CEREMONY

SANTA TIERRAS

Most of us who are conscious to living a sacred life devote a good deal of energy towards creating a comfortable sacred space within our homes. But we often forget to work with the spirit of the land on which our home resides—the santa tierra.

Working with the spirit of place is deeply supportive of your fulfillment while living in a particular location. For any of the other ceremonies that involve working with a santa tierra or local land spirit, this is the ceremony that will build your initial relationship of power. Having a close relationship with the spirit of your land will empower every single activity you perform in life. This is big and powerful work! Yet, like most ceremonies shared here, it is simple actions along with strong intention and unwavering commitment that get the job done.

My work with my santa tierra has delivered pure miracles in my life. From getting an over-asking price offer on my home in less than 3 days of being listed to finding & moving into a beautiful new home (that had everything on my wish list) in less than 24 hours of arriving in a new state, I cannot stress enough the power of having a strong relationship with the land.

This ceremony is like building an outdoor altar for your santa tierra. With all of our unique living situations, you may have to get creative. You can build this within a flower pot on a patio or even on your windowsill if you live in a high-rise apartment. As long as you place it somewhere that the connection to your land can be established, you will be in great shape!

MATERIALS

- Crystals, sticks, feathers, flowers, statues, etc. - anything you wish to place on your outdoor altar! Try to make sure some of the objects are strong enough to handle the elements of the changing seasons.

- Offerings from your medicine bag

THE CEREMONY

1. Awaken sacred space in the location where you will build your altar.
2. Creatively and beautifully arrange your objects in the space. Place each object with deep loving intention as an offering to your santa tierra.
3. Place offerings from your medicine bag on the altar.
4. Close sacred space when your altar is complete.

5. Refresh the offerings regularly to keep building the relationship with your santa tierra. I keep a medicine bag in my purse and sprinkle prayer filled offerings while walking to my car on my way out of the house. Remember your consistent commitment and you will most certainly feel your santa tierra show up when you call!

> *Indoors or outdoors, altars deserve regular attention! Keep the offerings fresh and remove any spent objects as needed. The more devotion in your practice, the more I believe the prayers placed on your altar will be heard!*

NOTES FOR YOUR OWN CEREMONY

NOURISH, TRANSFORM & HEAL

So many of us have such a challenging relationship with the foods that keep us nourished and alive. We have addictions, guilt, allergies, aversions, extreme diets... and on and on.

Much of our "baggage" around food is only present because we have completely disconnected from our earthly food connection. When it was a requirement to grow your own food and eat only with the seasons (as there were truly no other options) it was simple to stay in a state of gratitude for what you had and to enjoy each bite in both nourishment and pleasure.

Can we return this level of mindfulness and sacredness to our dinner tables? Can we re-establish a healthy relationship with our food and at the same time with pachamama? Can we heal through our foods, even if they are not what we assume are the healthiest, most extreme foods on the planet?

This work is very personal to me and is an essential practice. I spent 4 years eating an extremely strict 100% vegan, 100% organic, 100% raw food diet. I chose this path for healing and it worked. Since it worked so well, I really didn't feel inspired to change things up, which is why I stuck with it for so long.

But 4 years is a very long time to be the food outsider at every single social gathering... to eat cold foods even in the dead of winter... and to be strict to a fault, ultimately ending up nutritionally deficient.

So, I made the choice to introduce flexibility. I explored cooking with heat and eating what friends and family offered me (within reason, though I still choose to exclude meat, dairy and unnatural foods). I lived it up while traveling and enjoyed the ecstatic bliss of each bite.

But something unexpected happened in this shift. I felt guilty when I would stray a little too far, as if I wasn't allowed the pleasure and I wasn't treating my sacred body healthy enough. I noticed little allergy symptoms popping up here and there depending on what I ate. All of this, mind you, came along with food that most people would deem as very healthy—organic & vegan whole foods.

I knew what my mind was doing with these foods wasn't healthy at all and I took this awareness with me to Peru for healing. First, I had a soul retrieval for the physical symptoms and allergies I had to certain cooked foods. I don't know exactly what those bells or Quechua prayers awakened in me, or what was in that tea I was told to drink the next day, but my mindset totally shifted. That was some powerful medicine!

Later, in ceremony, there was a deeper message. The idea was presented to energetically shift both my body and my food at mealtime so that the body can take what it needs from food and let go of the rest, without issue.

And then there were the reminders of prayer. My shaman sister Loren asked if I had been praying with my meals, and indeed, this had long been forgotten.

All of this awakened in me a need for a simple ceremonial prayer that could be brought to each plate, making mealtime sacred, joyful, and healthy in its own way.

Below is my prayer. Feel free to use or adapt it and create your own. Hold your plate or food while speaking this prayer aloud to infuse your meal with the energy and intention of health and pleasure.

Whenever possible, include an offering along with your prayer. This can be as simple as placing a small pinch of the food you are about to enjoy on the earth.

THE PRAYER

Thank you, pachamama, for your unconditional nourishment. Please accept my love, reverence, and gratitude in return.

May this food nourish me in health and pleasure.

May each bite bring healing and strength.

May this food be medicine for my body, mind, and soul.

May I release all energies of this food that do not serve me with ease and swiftness.

Thank you, pachamama.

NOTES FOR YOUR OWN PRAYER

SOUL AWAKENING

Soul retrieval is a shamanic practice that I hold dear to my heart. In essence, it is a ceremony in which a shaman calls home parts of your soul… parts of your consciousness, parts of your vibrancy… that have left you or shut down during times of trauma. This loss can leave you feeling off course, broken, and confused.

As a receiver of this medicine, I have experienced other worldly transformations that I can barely explain. As a medicine carrier, this ceremony lights me up like no other, as I get to bear witness to such an intimate reawakening of a fully vibrant soul.

As powerful as this ceremony is, I have also witnessed spontaneous soul retrievals in clients while simply performing energy clearing work. It's as if we peeled back the layer of trauma that needed healing and a tender soul piece felt safe to shine once again. This supports the idea that soul retrieval is really a process of reawakening and there are many methods to reach the same goal.

I believe that there are times and circumstances under which we can provide this healing experience for ourselves. I would call this a "soul awakening" where we talk to our lost soul part and we call it back home with the utmost strength and clarity of intention.

This is a ceremony to accomplish just that—to do your own healing work, to call your lost soul part back home and to integrate it back into your life—in a sacred and joyful way.

This ceremony works best if you have already done some healing, clearing, and forgiveness work as necessary around the trauma, but still feel that something is missing from your essential self.

MATERIALS

- The recipe and ingredients to make your favorite food. Choose a dish that conjures up joyful memories. Perhaps this is something your grandmother used to make for you as a child or another nostalgic family recipe.

THE CEREMONY

1. Gather your ingredients and pre-measure them. Study your recipe so you can stay intentional in your food preparation process rather than get distracted with logistics.

2. Awaken sacred space in your kitchen. Share your intention of reawakening a lost part of your soul aloud.

3. Begin to prepare your food. With each chop, stir, addition of ingredients, etc., call to your soul part. Do this aloud if at all possible. Call him or her by your own name with love and sweetness. Let your soul piece know that he/she is safe to come home. It is safe to wake up. It is safe to shine vibrantly. It is safe to live in its fullest expression. Stay in this prayer the entire time you are preparing the food. If the food needs to bake, relax into meditation and continue the prayer as consistently as possible.

4. Make the final presentation of the dish as beautiful as possible. Remember that rather than a simple meal, this is a sacred ceremony. The strength of your intention to heal will be shown through your attention to detail and devotion to beauty.

5. When the food is complete, your final prayer and intention is that this dish is infused with your soul essence. Say this aloud.

6. When the food is ready to eat, sit consciously with your plate for a moment, saying a prayer, asking your soul piece to integrate and come to full life with each bite.

7. Enjoy your food with intention, gratitude, and pleasure—and without an ounce of distraction. As you digest and assimilate, the reawakening process will continue.

8. Watch your transformation over the next week and be gentle with yourself. Eat well and get plenty of rest. These tender parts need loving care when they return and must feel safe. So surround yourself with kind people and do what you love to keep your vibrant light shining!

NOTES FOR YOUR OWN CEREMONY

DEEP EARTH CONNECTION

Where many of us spend our days indoors, on computers, in cars, and rushing around, it's no surprise that we find ourselves feeling ungrounded and disconnected from the earthly rhythms we were designed to stay in sync with. Reconnecting and grounding into the earth is a practice and participating in ceremony is a very sweet way to strengthen our own roots.

I love connecting with large, old trees that seem to have the idea of balance all figured out. They are deeply rooted into the belly of pachamama, strong and stable. Yet, they still reach up into the sky above, growing closer and closer to the place of dreams and destinies.

Making a regular, intentional connection with a wise old tree and giving offerings to the spirit within connects us to those deep, strong roots. When making this a regular practice with the same tree, you can also develop another powerful relationship with an earth spirit that will support you on your path.

MATERIALS

- A local tree that calls to your heart & soul
- Flowers or other beautiful, biodegradable offerings

THE CEREMONY

1. Take a little time to explore your local land. Find a tree that really calls to you—one that makes you light up all over!

2. Awaken sacred space.

3. Make a beautiful offering to the spirit of this tree with strong intention to learn from its balanced and grounded ways.

4. When your offering is complete, sit quietly facing the tree in meditation. Close your eyes and visualize your energetic roots growing strong and deep, mirroring the roots of your chosen tree. Feel stable, supported, and strong. Then, visualize your energetic branches, reaching higher and higher, connecting you to your highest destiny. Feel the balance between your roots and branches, stable yet flexible in the flow of the breeze.

5. When you feel complete, close the space, thanking the tree for the connection you have made.

6. Make this a regular practice to stay deeply grounded and on your highest path!

NOTES FOR YOUR OWN CEREMONY

SACRED ENDINGS

Life is full of cycles. Just as a seed sprouts, grows into its full expression, produces its own seeds, then dies and returns to the earth, many phases of our lives come full circle through beginnings and endings. We have many ways to create ceremony around beginnings (weddings, baby showers, house warmings, etc.), but beyond the ceremonies held at death, we don't often bring the sacred to our endings.

Divorces or endings of friendships, losing or leaving a job, selling a house, or any other close to a cycle can be very important to acknowledge in the most sacred of ways. I believe it is important for us to ceremonially accept the blessings and lessons from the previous cycle as well as to release the challenges so we don't find them popping up in the next cycle to work through once again. Think about dating someone with the same short temper that drove you from your last relationship or taking a job with another boss who never gives promotions. No thanks! We so often find ourselves in repeating negative patterns when we haven't taken the time to do our healing work. That's where the magic of this ceremony lies. It clears the slate, giving us a completely fresh start to the next cycle.

MATERIALS

- Candles
- A lighter

THE CEREMONY

1. To decide how many candles you will need, take a moment to meditate on the individual challenges from this past cycle that you would like to release during this ceremony. You will need one candle for each challenge plus one extra.

2. Awaken sacred space in a darkened room.

3. Light all candles except for one and sit with the light surrounding you.

4. Each lit candle represents a challenge that you will be putting to rest at the end of this cycle. Assign each candle to a specified challenge.

5. Pick up one candle and allow yourself to feel the reality of this challenge. Feel it in your body, in your mind, and in your soul. How did it first come to be? How is it living within you now? What part of you needs healing in order to let it go? While holding the candle, use your intention to move this energy through your body, through your arms, through your hands, and right into the candle. Once you feel like you have moved the energy out of your body, blow out the candle.

6. Repeat this process until all candles are blown out.

7. Take the final candle that hasn't been lit yet. Focus on the blessings of this last cycle. Feel them as deeply as you felt the challenges and move that energy through your hands and into the candle. Once you feel that the candle has been infused with your blessings, light this last candle with the intention of carrying these blessings forth into the next cycle. Sit with this candle in meditation for a few moments.

8. Close your sacred space and blow out the final candle.

9. After a week or so, once the energy from this ceremony settles, you may want to try a Despacho Ceremony (page 26) or Destiny Lines (page 50) to plant the seeds and intentions of your next cycle.

NOTES FOR YOUR OWN CEREMONY

DESTINY LINES

I absolutely love working in the realm of destiny. In my eyes, it's as if we are born with the seeds of our highest destinies and then these seeds are activated and begin to sprout in the perfect moment. I've seen it in my own life so many times. Divine inspiration will strike in a way that totally rocks my world, but it will show up in such a way that I ask: "how could I possibly have not thought of this before?". Then, I smile, and remember that this is the perfect moment to take a leap, not a day sooner, not a day later.

But what happens when our lives have been challenging to the point of losing this connection? Sometimes traumas leave our inner landscape barren without the energy to germinate these sacred seeds. Or, we miss the inspiration, the sprouting phase, with fear and old patterns standing in the way of taking that necessary first step.

This ceremony is about activating your highest destiny. It is a ceremony of re-fertilization, sprouting, and growing into your fullest expression. It was created for those times in life when you feel lost and disconnected from your life's purpose. It brings a sacred intention to realigning your soul with the completely unique and essential reason for living your life now.

MATERIALS

- A plant that is grown from large seeds (for example, sunflowers)
- Many seeds from the type of plant chosen above (for example, sunflower seeds)
- A journal & pen

THE CEREMONY

1. Awaken sacred space in the place you will work. Set your intention to connect with and sprout the seeds of your highest destiny.

2. Take a handful of seeds and with the breath of your prayer, blow your intention to connect with your destiny right into the seeds. Begin to create a sacred pathway with the seeds in any shape you like. Place your prayers into every handful of seeds, through your breath. Make the path long enough that you could walk at least a few steps.

3. At the end of the path, you will place the fully grown plant. Again, use your breath to infuse the plant with your prayers. This plant represents the full expression of your destiny, so use the intention that it will be revealed to you.

4. Create a mantra that you will repeat while walking the path. It should express your intention to activate your highest destiny simply and beautifully. Sit with your journal and make some notes until it feels just right. My mantra is:

> *"My highest destiny is clear to me and I am living it now".*

5. Walk the path with bare feet, feeling the seeds beneath you, at least 10 times, back and forth. As you walk, repeat your mantra. Keep walking until you feel a shift.

6. When you feel complete with walking the path, sit at the end with the plant and the path in front of your body. Bring the plant into your belly, touching it there, while using your intention to infuse your energy body with the spark of activation that you have created during this ceremony. Repeat the same process with your heart and then with your third eye.

7. Once complete with the ceremony, you may wish to journal a bit and share any inspiration that came. Being in a ceremonial state connects us more deeply to our intuition, so it wouldn't be unlikely to finish up with some hints of where to take your next step.

8. Stay awake over the next few weeks to the sprouting of your seeds. You may feel drawn to try something new or you may remember something that you have been longing to do since childhood. These destiny hints are powerful and should come as no surprise when you have used such strong intention in a ceremony like this one.

NOTES FOR YOUR CEREMONY & MANTRA

GROWING FORGIVENESS

Forgiveness is such a rich topic. For many of us, it is one of life's greatest challenges. The events that need to be forgiven can bind us down tighter than anything. The blessing comes when we realize how much freedom true forgiveness can offer, but the curse lies in the challenge to fully and unconditionally let go and find this peace.

When we are working through exceptionally dark moments, there isn't always something tangible that can be done to move us along our healing journey with more speed. Forgiveness takes time—like the healing of a wound—a soul needs mending and allowance to go through its own process of regeneration.

This is where the gift of ceremony comes in. I see it like a big dose of vitamin C for the soul. In my work, ceremony is a mega boost to the soul's immune and repair system.

Whether you have been hurt by another or you are longing to forgive yourself, ceremony is key in strengthening your progress. This ceremony was created to give your healing process an energetic boost, while still acknowledging the time involved to find ultimate forgiveness.

This ceremony has a bit of flexibility built into it, depending on the time of year and the climate you live in, so adapt as necessary, while keeping the same rock solid intent.

MATERIALS

- A place to dig in the dirt and bury some objects. Wherever you choose, make sure it is a place you can check in with from time to time. If the climate or time of year is not conducive to digging and sprouting seeds, you may need to wait to complete the full ceremony, or you can choose to only perform the releasing portion.

- A small shovel

- Items you wish to bury. This is very personal, but my recommendation would be papers with thoughts on what you wish to forgive, your written intention for the final outcome, objects that may link you to the person you wish to forgive, etc.

- Seeds that sprout easily or a young plant

THE CEREMONY

1. Awaken sacred space in your chosen location.

2. Prepare all of your materials for burying. Use very strong intention when writing out your thoughts on forgiveness. Any tangible objects should be infused with your breath and prayer.

3. Dig a hole several inches deep. Each time you dig, call on pachamama to help you release your pain and the attachment to your story. Call on her assistance for unconditional forgiveness.

4. One by one, place the prayer filled objects into the hole. Once they are all placed, say a final prayer or intention for your ultimate forgiveness.

5. Begin to return dirt to the hole, covering the objects. As you do this, you again ask pachamama to infuse your spirit with the ability to forgive.

6. Place the seeds at their recommended depth, and plant them according to the instructions. Alternately, if you can't sprout seeds now, just keep burying the objects until the hole is completely covered.

7. Water the seeds if necessary and continue to do so as required, with the intention of bringing full life to your forgiveness each and every time.

8. If you weren't able to plant seeds, plant something already living at the site of your ceremony as soon as you are able. The idea is that the sprouts or plant will grow over time as your forgiveness process becomes more and more complete. This ceremony gives great intention to the release, but also respects the need for healing time through the growth of a plant.

9. When your plant has matured, your soul shall mirror back inner peace.

10. Close sacred space whenever your ceremony feels complete to you.

NOTES FOR YOUR OWN CEREMONY

MOON MAMA

I've had some pretty remarkable experiences when working in ceremony under the light of the moon. I created this ceremony for women to deepen the connection of their monthly rhythms with that of Mama Killa or grandmother moon herself.

Let me share a story.

A couple of years back, my moon cycle was all out of whack. I hadn't changed anything in my diet or lifestyle, I wasn't under any new stress, and I just couldn't figure out what was going on. I couldn't find a physical connection, so I took my desire to return to my natural rhythm as a need for spiritual work.

I thought of the moon as she pulls on the tides and guides our monthly cycles. And of course, I thought of ceremony as my tool for healing. On the night of the full moon, I lit a fire and made offerings to her under the radiant, glowing light. I prayed to reconnect and re-sync our rhythms as one. I had a beautiful energetic dialogue of giving and receiving with her that night.

As beautiful as this ceremony was, I was still a little humbled by the outcome—extremely grateful—but humbled nonetheless. My next cycle completely re-routed itself and started up at the new moon and has since remained in predictable rhythm. If that wasn't a testament to the power of ceremony for me, I don't know what would be!

This ceremony is for all women who wish to build a deep relationship with grandmother moon so that you can call on her when your body is in need, knowing she will always answer.

My preference is to do this ceremony on the night of full moon when her energy is very strong.

MATERIALS

- Bunches of white flowers

THE CEREMONY

1. Choose a time of day and location where you can see the moon. Awaken sacred space in the place you wish to work.

2. Pick up your flowers and infuse them with your prayers through your breath. Share your strong intention of communion with the moon and of connecting your rhythm with her own.

3. Create a path with the white flowers between you and the moon, linking your spirits.

4. Sit quietly with your intention, gazing at the moon, and feeling the connection grow and strengthen.

5. Pick up the flowers closest to you and bring them to your belly with the intention of weaving the moon's energy into your own energy body. Repeat this process at your heart and then at your third eye.

6. Leave the flowers as an offering to the moon.

7. Close sacred space when you're ready.

8. Pay attention to how your cycle shifts over the next month. Repeat the ceremony monthly until you feel like you have established a very deep connection. Once the connection is made, maintain it with regular offerings on the new and full moon, and perhaps at the beginning of your own cycle.

NOTES FOR YOUR OWN CEREMONY

SACRED WORKSPACE

Creating an altar is a powerful ceremony in itself. It may seem simple, but it is a tool I turn to time and time again. I love creating fresh altars with intentions at the new moon, altars to heal specific challenges in my life, and altars to support other people who have asked me for prayers.

I have little sacred altars set up all over my home and I keep them fresh, dusted, and ever changing so the energy never gets stale or forgotten. One of the most important places for me to have sacred, intentional objects is at my workspace.

Whether you work for yourself or for a large corporation, I'm certain you have goals and dreams that could use some support from spirit. We all do! You might be going for a promotion, working on a stressful deadline, or even hoping to leave your current job to follow a greater calling. Whatever it is, I highly recommend setting up a little sacred space for manifesting and visioning at work. We spend so much time and energy at our jobs, it really isn't the place for us to forget working with spirit.

Of course, this will have to adapt to your unique work situation. I can imagine awakening sacred space with my bells and rattle in the communal office I used to work in and that vision is not pretty. But even if you don't have a desk job with a private office, you can make it work! Are you a flight attendant? Keep a small wooden box filled with sacred objects in your suitcase. Are you on the road all the time? Make the altar in your car. With a little flexibility and creativity, you'll find your way.

MATERIALS

- A journal & pen for notes
- Any objects that are sacred to you: crystals, images, small figures, feathers, sticks, stones, candles, flowers, herbs... your choice!

THE CEREMONY

1. Please adapt this ceremony as necessary to make it comfortable for your working situation. You can even begin it at home — awakening sacred space and praying into your objects. Then, you can casually but intentionally set them up at work. Trust your own inner guide to run the show on this one.
2. Awaken sacred space.

3. Take some time to focus on your work and career based intentions. Write them out and refine them to a handful of your most present and important goals.

4. Gather enough objects so each intention can be assigned to its own item.

5. Working one by one, use your breath and your prayers to infuse each object with your intent.

6. Arrange the objects in your space, moving them here and there until it feels just right.

7. Lay out some sort of offering for spirit, be it flowers, herbs, or a sprinkle from your medicine bag (page 19). Infuse your offering with your breath of gratitude for the support spirit is giving your goals.

8. Say a closing prayer of thanks, but you can ask spirit to remain at your altar as your goals begin to take form.

9. Remember to keep your altar clean and sacred! Dust it and change out the objects as things manifest and new goals arise. Just don't ignore it!

NOTES FOR YOUR OWN CEREMONY

MAKING MEDICINE

Ceremony is all about intention. It is the strength of the intention that truly shifts things. If you are working to heal something within your physical body, a daily intentional prayer or ceremony can support you both in your faith and healing process. Through this particular ceremony, we can create our own energetic medicine to boost the body's inherent ability to heal.

When we really want big and lasting change, I find that consistency is key. If you're looking to heal something chronic or more serious, creating one intention or one ceremony doesn't really convey our commitment to spirit. For this reason, I wanted to create a simple ceremony to assist the body in healing that would be sustainable to perform every single day.

We are all busy, but when you are truly ready to heal, you have to commit to taking immaculate care of yourself. Make this ceremony a testament to your commitment and I believe spirit will reciprocate and support your process.

MATERIALS

- A glass jar
- Pure water
- Fruits & herbs to infuse the water (even better to use healing herbs or medicinal tinctures)

THE CEREMONY

1. Awaken sacred space and call on spirit to aid in your healing.
2. Intentionally prepare all of your fruits and herbs.
3. Pray over your ingredients as you add each one to the jar. Create a prayer that powerfully embodies your intention for healing.
4. Fill the jar with water.
5. Pray over the entire jar. Make your prayer strong and say it out loud. Ask for this water to become your medicine. Ask that it be infused with the healing power of spirit. Ask that it nourish and cleanse your body. Ask that it give you clear vision to see where your next step on the healing path lies. Add any other personal prayers.

> *When we really want big and lasting change, I find that consistency is key. If you're looking to heal something chronic or more serious, creating one intention or one ceremony doesn't really convey our commitment to spirit.*

6. Close sacred space.

7. Take the water with you and drink it throughout the day, remembering that this is your sacred medicine and that you are healing with every sip.

NOTES FOR YOUR OWN CEREMONY

CELEBRATING LOVE

It is my belief that those of us who are blessed enough to be in joyful, supportive, soul-connected partnerships have an obligation to regularly celebrate in gratitude! This is never something to be taken for granted.

My go-to celebration ceremonies are mandalas (page 104) and despachos (page 26). These are both wonderful to share with your partner on anniversaries and other special days. But if you'd like to try something a little more unique, I created this ceremony for a little extra intention.

This ceremony is about creating a living, wearable altar that is ever growing as a tribute to your love for one another. It is a symbol of the evolution of your relationship and its increasing strength.

It is ideal to revisit this ceremony year after year on anniversaries, but it doesn't have to be limited to one day per year. It can be turned to if times get tough and you are longing for reconnection. Or it can be shared on a seemingly random day when you just feel like celebrating the joys of love.

There is a lot of flexibility here based on what you wish to create. You can choose a necklace, bracelet, anklet, earrings, or even a key chain if you don't like wearing jewelry.

MATERIALS

- Strings, beads, charms, jewelry clasps, etc., or anything else needed to create the pieces you and your partner desire. Part of the celebration can be looking for jewelry inspiration and shopping for materials together.

THE CEREMONY

1. Remember that this will be an evolving piece, so it can be helpful to lay out some sort of plan, leaving space to add items over the years. You may create something simple and add one bead per year. Or you may wish to create a large, statement piece, adding an entire new strand each time you work on it. Or you may create a full piece and just add a new charm at each celebration. The choice is yours!

2. Awaken sacred space where you will be working together.

3. Have a sweet conversation about the love, energy, wishes, and gratitude you want to infuse into this piece. When you have refined your prayers, use your breath to infuse them into your objects.

> *Ceremony isn't just about fixing things. It's about celebrating & intentionally expressing gratitude for the parts of life that are working. When we enter the space of celebration, I believe we are just attracting more & more of this sweetness.*

4. Intentionally craft your pieces together. Keep your mind focused on your prayers as every step builds a stronger and stronger energetic charge in your loving creation. It is fun to try to keep your eyes off of the piece your partner is creating for you so it can be a surprise!

5. When the pieces are complete, infuse each full creation with one more love filled breath.

6. Take turns putting the pieces on each other as you exchange loving words.

7. Close sacred space.

8. Keep revisiting and building these pieces together whenever you get the chance. Love is so worth celebrating!

NOTES FOR YOUR OWN CEREMONY

MAKING SPACE FOR MONEY

Money is such a tricky, sticky subject. There are so many beliefs around it, some that are beneficial and many that are not. There are sweet sayings like "do what you love and the money will follow" which make us feel warm and fuzzy, but from a shamanic perspective, we can't just stop there. If you have misaligned energy towards accepting or attracting money, some of these miracles may feel way out of reach. To bridge that gap, it may require that we work a little ceremonial magic.

In the culture of the Q'ero, at the heart of all life is ayni, or sacred reciprocity. If our needs to receive are not being met, we must explore if we are living in ayni. We may be giving too much or too little. We may be taking more than we need or ignoring our own needs. In either scenario, we find ourselves way out of balance and in situations that are less than ideal.

This ceremony is about pressing a metaphorical reset button on the financial front. It's about making energetic space for receiving money. It also gives you the opportunity to explore and really refine your financial goals. Altogether, the goal of this ceremony is to realign your soul with a healthy balance of giving and receiving in sacred reciprocity.

You will likely need to work with this ceremony over multiple days. Enjoy each moment of the process, knowing that with sacred commitment and forward action, you will see results.

MATERIALS

- A journal & pen
- Space to build an altar
- Objects for the altar that symbolize financial abundance

THE CEREMONY

1. Awaken and close sacred space each time you work within this ceremony.

2. The first stage of this resetting process is to deeply explore your financial goals. This isn't about creating some dreamy, one in a million chance situation. This is the time to think about your next year or so and see what is a true potential that you can pray on, believe in, and take action steps towards. Perhaps you've always dreamed of being a multimillionaire. But have you considered the responsibility that would come along with it? Would it bring more ease or more stress into your life? Is there a more attainable, short term goal that would make you just as happy, if not more? Take some time with your journal and write what comes through with the aid of spirit.

3. Refine your goals into 3 or fewer clearly written statements of intention.

FINANCIAL INTENTIONS

1.

2.

3.

4. Next, we must make space for receiving by getting rid of clutter and belongings that we do not need. This could be a small project or a huge one depending on how often you may engage in this purging practice. But I highly recommend it for making change! The more you do this, it the easier it gets and the better it feels. It not only opens your energy up to receive, it also clears out any stale energy from your sacred home space.

So what exactly must we do? Go through all of your belongings. Dig through closets, the basement, the garage and the attic. Likely, we all have a ton of stuff that we simply do not need at all. Some of it is held onto for "just in case" moments and this increases a lack mentality that I find does not help us to attract money. It's part of the overall misalignment that we are trying to heal. No matter how many times I have done this, I am always amazed at how much more I can find to pass along.

Make piles of things you are willing to donate and things that would be salable. Depending on what you end up with, you may wish to have a yard sale or go the internet sales route. Either way, you are freeing up some crucial energetic space.

I know this practice is easy for some and extremely difficult for others. If you need it, call on a loved one for help; someone who is great at prioritizing and organizing and has a lot of compassion! I have gone through this many, many times and I know that the first time was the absolute hardest. But now, I love to do regular purges. I donate to organizations I feel great about helping and sell some higher ticket items. Completing this process with money in your pocket is what this ceremony is all about! How's that for instant results?!

5. Finally, I find it important to build an altar for the three goals you refined above. Find a space in your newly cleaned home to dedicate towards your sacred money prayers. Write your intentions on strips of paper for the altar or assign each intention to an object and place them on the altar. Bring candles and other offerings to spirit at this place of prayer. Visit with it at least once a day, restating your intentions as prayers to spirit. Refresh the offerings regularly. Make sure the intentions still hold up over time and if not, change them to reflect your current goals. Continue this practice until your financial state has transformed in the way you desire. At that point, shift into a gratitude practice.

NOTES FOR YOUR OWN CEREMONY

BURN IT UP

My favorite way to bring quick, radical change is with the assistance of the fire spirit. When I want to stop something dead in its tracks or close a door once and for all, I use a fire ceremony to release my energetic attachment and burn it right up!

What parts of your life would you like to leave behind today, once and for all? What can you release and burn off for a brighter tomorrow? What pain and trauma can be let go so you may rise up from the ashes in strength and power? These are the energies we want to bring to the fire.

The fire ceremony is one I return to regularly. Sometimes, a fire works a quick and painless miracle. Other times, we burn off the residue layer by layer. As you've learned, healing takes commitment and sometimes we need to work with the fire regularly to create lasting results. We can use this ceremony to create a reciprocal relationship with the spirit of fire. Over time, I know you will start to notice the amazing transformation this element can bring to your life.

MATERIALS

- A method to build a nice, safe outdoor fire, such as a fire pit. Follow proper fire safety techniques.

- Your medicine bag, a small despacho or another gift or offering for the fire. Let the beauty of your gift show your strong intention for healing.

- Paper and a pen

THE CEREMONY

1. Awaken sacred space in the location you will work.

2. Meditate on what you wish to release through this fire ceremony. Once you are very clear, write it on your paper in clear detail. While you write, allow the energy of your challenge to move through your body, through your energy field, through your hand, and on to the paper. The more you connect your energetic attachment with what you are writing, the more powerful this ceremony will be for you. It's likely that your focus on this challenge will bring up some anxiety, fear, or pain as you work with it.

Although it may feel uncomfortable, this is good medicine. You are bringing the energy close to the surface which makes it much easier to move and clear completely. When we are not willing to look at these things and truly feel them—when we leave them deep beneath the surface—this is when our work takes years and years. If you want to work quickly and completely, allow yourself to feel the waves of emotion and grief that naturally appear in this realm of soul work.

3. Once this process is complete and you have your energy filled paper, build and light your fire. Call on the spirit of fire to join you as you watch the flames grow strong.

4. Sit in prayer and in intention. Choose your own way to honor the fire while you express your intention of what you are releasing. You may choose to read your paper aloud, or you may summarize in a short, clear prayer. This is your choice.

5. Bring a gift to the fire as your offering. Use your breath to infuse the gift with a strong prayer of gratitude for the fire's healing powers. Place the gift in the fire and let it burn.

6. Once you feel that your gift has been accepted and it has burned completely, you may begin to work with the fire for your releasing ceremony. Sit, stand, or kneel safely, close to the fire.

7. Hold your paper in your hands and bring one last breath of energy to pull out any last threads of this challenge from within you. Let the paper be a sacred, healing vessel to capture the remains and hold them safe. When you are ready, intentionally place the paper, pulsing with energy, into the fire and let it burn completely.

8. Once your paper has completely turned to ash, use your hands to intentionally wave the element of fire into your belly, your heart, and your third eye. This practice brings power and determination into your soul so you may rise up and move forward with the support of spirit. Remember, this is intentional and you aren't actually touching the fire.

9. Once complete, sit with the fire in quiet reflection while it finishes burning. Say a few words of gratitude to the spirit of the fire.

10. Close sacred space and make sure your fire is completely out before leaving it.

NOTES FOR YOUR OWN CEREMONY

THE BEAUTY OF GRATITUDE

Light & dark.
High & low.
Up & down.
Joy & sorrow.

If there's one thing we can count on in life, we know that we will experience both the sweetness and the bitterness throughout our years on earth. We work to create a life that is overflowing with happiness and pray that the moments of grief are very few and far between.

A practice of celebrating gratitude and the goodness of life is something that I have always loved. I have often kept notes in a simple journal to cherish the sweetest moments, whether simple or grand. And when times were challenging, returning to review these sacred lists would help keep me from spiraling too deep into the darkness, remembering that the light always returned.

Thinking ceremonially, I wanted to create a gratitude practice that stood a little stronger than being tucked away in a pretty journal. I wanted to create something both visually beautiful and energetically powerful. The practice of gratitude should be an expression of prayers for what you want to create more of in life. This ceremony aligns you with celebrating and attracting more of the good.

MATERIALS

- A large jar
- A selection of smooth flat rocks, large enough to write on, but small enough to fit in your jar
- Fine point paint pens

THE CEREMONY

1. Awaken sacred space with your intention of gratitude and celebrating the beauty of life.
2. Select a few of your favorite stones.
3. Connect with your gratitude for life! What are some of the most wonderful things happening for you right now?

4. Assign each item of gratitude to an individual stone. Write a few words on each stone to represent your thoughts. You can use pictures too, if you like to draw and want some variety within your jar. You don't need to fill the jar on your first day. The idea is that you will begin with a few stones and continually add more over time.

5. One by one, place the stones in the jar with the intention of inviting more sweetness and joy into your life.

6. Close sacred space.

7. Continue to visit with the jar and add more sacred gratitude stones, at least once a week to keep this energy alive! This jar is like an altar within itself, and we don't want to leave it to be ignored.

8. When you fill your jar, you can begin another or move to a larger jar. The power is in seeing just how much beauty there truly is in life and how this continues to grow over the years. And when times are tough, dump out the jar and read your stones. Do your best to realign with these beautiful moments and remember that more are to come.

NOTES FOR YOUR OWN CEREMONY

RETURNING TO NOW

Much of our stress and worry is attached to the past or future. It is actually much more rare to be anxious about the present moment. Sure, we all have experiences of intense stress in times of crisis, deadlines and responsibility. But in our day to day life, more often than not, we are worrying about something that lies ahead or questioning something that happened in our past. If we can truly connect to the present moment, we can usually find peace and gratitude. We find that our needs are being met and all is well.

There are plenty of meditative practices that can deepen our connection to the present moment. But what can we call upon when we aren't in a place where we can drop everything, close our eyes, and just breathe?

This ceremony awakens your connection to the peace of the present moment. It creates a sensory association with that essential feeling so you can summon it even in the most stressful moments. Smelling particular scents can powerfully evoke memories, emotions, and states of being. I'm sure you've experienced this in your life before. Using this wisdom, we can create our own new connection, linking the feelings of tranquility that arise when we are truly present with a beautiful scent that will allow these feelings to resurface whenever this smell is near.

Creating the association from a scent to an emotion will take a dedicated practice. But once the bond is created, this will soon become your quickest and easiest method of quieting your anxious mind in any moment.

MATERIALS

- A journal & pen
- A rattle or drum
- An essential oil with a scent you enjoy, but one that you don't use or already have an association with. Ideally it would be brand new to you and would be a scent that is known to relax and elicit peace rather than uplift and excite.

THE CEREMONY

1. Set your intention and be clear about your commitment to creating your scent association. You will likely need to practice this at least a few times a week for a good solid month before the link will click. I know this sounds intense, but isn't changing your life worth it?

2. Each time you sit for this ceremony and meditation, awaken sacred space when you begin and close sacred space when you are complete.

3. Find a quiet and comfortable place to sit. If you can be outside, even better.

4. Begin by journaling, making notes about experiences that connect you to the present moment. Perhaps it is being in nature, laughing with friends, dancing, etc. We all have something that pulls us out of our minds and fully into the now.

5. Capture this initial feeling of presence by visualizing yourself in one of these experiences. Close your eyes, breathe fully and evenly, and begin creating a steady rhythm with the rattle or drum. Step into the day dream as if it is happening right now.

6. Let the visualization drift away when you are ready and begin to just focus on your breath and the sound of your rhythm. Feel the earth beneath you, supporting your physical body. Sink in and relax.

7. Feel the peace of this present moment. If thoughts arise, connect them to your exhale and push them aside. Let your focus return to the breath and the rhythm. If you are truly focusing on your breathing and keeping a steady rhythmic pace with the rattle or drum, you will stay completely out of your thoughts.

8. Find the sweet spot of peace and presence. When you feel that your have it and have held it steady for at least a few minutes, pull out your scent, place a drop in your hand, and breathe deeply. Take it all in and use your intention to connect this scent to your current calm and relaxed state of presence.

9. Put the scent away, return to a regular breath, and open your eyes when you are ready. Take a few moments to connect to the earth and feel grounded before moving and returning to your day.

10. Wash your hands well and do not touch your scent again until you are able to repeat this practice. You do not want to create associations between this scent and anything else.

11. Once you have practiced this regularly for at least a month, begin to carry the scent with you. When you notice a time of stress, anxiety and worry beginning to surface, place a drop of the oil in your hands and breath deeply. With strong intention, you should begin calming your thoughts immediately. The beauty of this is that you have already done the meditative work, so you can receive the benefits quickly anytime and anywhere.

12. Once the association is locked in, I suggest still visiting with the meditation once a week so that you keep it strong and to prevent creating a new association with your scent if you are only pulling it out in times of stress.

NOTES FOR YOUR OWN CEREMONY

days at the
un kisses
into the pleas
rine dds
g walk
 ll
 end

 the ocean

SIMPLIFICATION

Throughout my life, I have come to notice that the people I see living the simplest lives are also the most authentically happy. I'm sure you've seen it, too. Especially when visiting other cultures, you will observe people with very little money working quite simple professions, all while radiating the most genuine joy from their hearts that you have ever experienced.

Bearing witness to this has since inspired my every move. It has helped me whittle down my life in all regards. From purging unnecessary material goods to cutting back on excessive responsibilities, I have dramatically decreased my stress while massively increasing my happiness.

We all have things that we can let go of to lighten our energetic load. Many of us feel responsible for things that really shouldn't be our burden. Others have the tendency to give excessively while draining energy that is needed for themselves. Sometimes it is our own destructive thoughts or challenging belief systems that drain our vitality and create an overwhelming existence. No matter what it is for you, this ceremony is for releasing the weight of your burdens and making space for a much simpler, happier life.

This ceremony will likely need to be performed multiple times if you end up with a long list of things you wish to release. In the days following your ceremony, you may feel that your connection to some things has lightened dramatically while others are still present. After a couple of weeks, take those items that have remained heavy back to this ceremony. Continue repeating until you feel all the shifts you have hoped for.

MATERIALS

- Flowers (one flower for each item you wish to release)
- A location with a body of moving water that you can comfortably stand in

THE CEREMONY

1. Awaken sacred space in your waterside location, calling on the spirit of water to support you in letting go and simplifying.
2. Take a moment to collect your thoughts and list out each item that you wish to release during this ceremony.
3. Gather your flowers.
4. Step into the water.

5. Connect deeply to one burden you wish to shed. Feel how it lives within you and how it takes up space and energy within your life. Take one flower and use your breath to infuse it with the essence of your burden.

6. Place the flower in the water by your feet. Feel the water washing over you, cleansing any heaviness and washing it away.

7. Repeat this process for each item you are working with on this day.

8. Once complete, stay a few moments just feeling the water drawing out any last bits of stress and weight.

9. Step out of the water and close your sacred space with gratitude to the spirit of the water that you worked with today.

NOTES FOR YOUR OWN CEREMONY

CALMING THE STORM

This ceremony is akin to Simplification and Returning to Now, but was created more for the stressful realities of life that we can't necessarily drop. There are responsibilities that we must show up for that bring us great amounts of stress—like getting your kids ready for school in a rushed morning flurry or working to complete a work project with an unrealistic deadline.

Rather than just running away from it all when we have already committed and other people are counting on us, we can use this ceremony to draw some of the stressful energy out of our daily triggers and change our relationship to them.

This ceremony calls on Pachamama's (mother earth's) power to take the weight of our burdens and transform their energetic charge so we no longer view them in the same way. This helps us to meet each challenge with more peace, feeling supported in our lives, even if that support is only showing up from spirit or Pachamama.

If you can take the time to visit this ceremony once a month, I am quite certain that each time you show up, your list of stressors is going to get smaller and smaller. Your strong intention and your connection to the earth are the master keys to making this happen!

MATERIALS

- A journal & pen
- Your medicine bag from Embodying Sacred Reciprocity
- Small stones (quantity to be determined by how many stressors you are working with)
- Leaves (quantity to be determined by how many stressors you are working with)
- A small shovel or trowel
- An outdoor space for your ceremony where you can dig small holes to bury your stones.

THE CEREMONY

1. Begin by awakening sacred space. Be particularly intentional in calling Pachamama and the santa tierras (the spirits of the land). This is who you want showing up to support you in this transformation!

2. Use your journal to make notes about the things in your life that are causing you the most stress. Try to refine your list down to 6 or less major stressors.

3. Dig a small hole in the earth for each item from your list that you wish to drain the stress from.

4. Place a stone in front of each hole.

5. Begin with the first stone, holding it in your hand and sitting down in a comfortable position. Close your eyes and breathe deeply to relax your body. Connect with the energy and emotion behind your first stressor. Does it make you sad, angry, anxious, etc.? Where in your body do you feel the emotions rise? Connect the energy that you've located to your breath. Once the intentional connection has been made, breathe into the stone. Breathe your prayer of releasing the stress, releasing the emotion, and releasing the energy.

6. Place the stone in the first hole and place a small offering from your medicine bag on top of it. This offering is a gift to pachamama. Infuse it with your breath of intention and gratitude for her willingness to help you drain and transform your stress.

7. Bury the stone and the offerings in the earth.

8. Top the buried items with a leaf and another sprinkling of offerings. This time, your offerings and prayer are a gift to the santa tierras —the local land spirits. Your gift is an exchange for the transformational power that the land spirits can offer you in this moment. Again, use your breath to infuse the offerings with your strongest intentions and gratitude.

9. Sit on the earth with your line of offerings in front of you. Spend a few quiet and intentional moments feeling the earth draw any heavy energy from your body, taking it deeper and deeper beneath the surface. Let it go and leave it behind.

10. When you feel an unquestionable lightness, you may close your sacred space, expressing your most heartfelt thanks to pachamama and the santa tierras.

NOTES FOR YOUR OWN CEREMONY

CALLING IN LOVE

Nearly every person I have crossed paths with has held the deep desire for true, loving partnership. From sharing in life's beauty to having support during the most challenging times, partnership is one of the greatest gifts and pleasures of the human experience. Yet, for many, a meaningful and healthy partnership remains as elusive and out of reach as the stars in the sky.

Love seems to come so easy for some while it is the greatest challenge for others and we can't always understand why this is. Therefore, when you seek out love, you must align yourself from multiple angles, exploring and committing to all of the facets of bringing love to life. I have created this particular ceremony to leave no stone unturned, combining prayer, offerings, commitment, and energetic connection to birth a miracle.

Your prayer is twofold. Number one, you have to heal and clear any energetic blockages to love and partnership. These blockages make us almost invisible to potential lovers until the fog has lifted. Number two, you must be very clear about who you are inviting. You don't want just anyone showing up at your door with roses.

Your offerings are your exchange. We never pray and receive without giving. We live in ayni, in sacred reciprocity.

Your deep commitment is reflected back to you in what shows up. Your commitment to consistent prayer and offerings of exchange will change everything.

Your energetic connection is likely the most important piece. You are going to be deepening a relationship and praying to the spirit of your local land—your santa tierra. Luckily, your santa tierra has access and a connection to all of the santa tierras around the globe. This means that your santa tierra can share your prayers with the santa tierra of the partner you are inviting. It's like passing a note to your best friend to ask your crush to meet you on the playground after school. The respective santa tierras makes the initial connection and this is exactly where the magic happens.

Are you ready?

MATERIALS

- A gorgeous piece of rose quartz that you resonate with deeply
- Your medicine bag for offerings plus fresh flowers and other gifts as desired

THE CEREMONY

1. To begin this ceremony, you will first need to find a place to work. Look within your local landscape for a tree, a rock, a flower bed... a sacred symbol of your local santa tierra. Find a place you are comfortable visiting every day and able to leave offerings that will ideally remain untouched.

2. Choose a day to begin this committed practice. It may take a few days, or it may take a year to bring love into your life, depending on your healing process. So, pick a time that establishing a new, regular practice will work for your schedule.

3. Bring your rose quartz and offerings to your chosen location and awaken sacred space.

4. Sit with the rose quartz in your hands and close your eyes. You want to infuse this crystal with your greatest prayer for love. This includes prayers for healing your blockages or old love wounds and your prayers for inviting in your new partner. The rose quartz is the pinnacle of your offerings, so please take your time with this, being crystal clear with your wording and intention. Once you have your prayer, use your breath to infuse these words into the stone. Place the stone somewhere where it will be safe for your santa tierra, even if this means burying it in the ground. Make it very clear that this is a gift for the spirit of your land.

5. Add other offerings in beauty and intention.

6. Return to this place daily in prayer and offering. This will flow in a unique cycle depending on your own personal journey. You may need months of prayer to clear blockages. Make that your strong prayer as you leave your offerings. You may need to spend a week or more praying to heal the damage of one painful relationship wound. This will of course vary for everyone. But check in with yourself and ask your santa tierra for help: "what do I need in order to make myself fully open and available to true partnership?". Listen for her answer and follow her lead. She is your guide in all of this. Keep working for your healing until you feel a shift.

7. When you feel clear, whether it's been a day or six months, your focus can change. If you are unsure of your timing for changing gears, again, your santa tierra will guide you. Look for signs that your santa tierra leaves when you are ready. Perhaps there is a new flower that has just bloomed. Maybe a bird dropped a feather as a message from spirit. Be aware, look, and listen.

8. Your daily visit for prayers and offerings should now carry the intention of asking your santa tierra to reach out to the santa tierra of your ideal partner. It may help to revisit the qualities of the person you are praying for. This may have changed over time as you have been going through your healing process and have been given access to greater awareness.

9. Again, be consistent with your prayers and offerings. Feel the presence of love draw closer everyday. Let your santa tierra guide and inspire you. Where will this meeting take place? Let her arrange for you to be in the right place at the right time.

10. It is my recommendation to continue this practice until love arrives. And even at that point, it would be beneficial to bring weekly prayers of gratitude. Your santa tierra has worked some major magic and it is not fair to forget her! You may close sacred space in ceremony when the time is right. But continue to visit your santa tierra for other ceremonies and give her regular offerings. She is an extremely powerful ally for all facets of your life—not just in love!

> *One note on this ceremony: if there is someone in particular you are trying to create a relationship with, remember the shamanic philosophy on permission, shared in the introduction of this guide. Please work with the highest level of ethics and do not attempt to create anything for anyone who has not given you permission. I recommend completing this ceremony without attachment to a particular person for the highest outcome.*

NOTES FOR YOUR OWN CEREMONY

SACRED CELEBRATION

I am the kind of person who likes to celebrate anything and everything. It's always been important to me to recognize the beauty and accomplishments of life. No matter the occasion, for me, it's always been about joyful recognition with good food and great company.

These days, I also adore bringing a ceremonial layer to my celebrations. For me, it adds to the sacredness and creates deeper meaning and sweeter memories.

As a gift to the person being celebrated, I love to create nature based mandalas in exquisite beauty and highest intention. Mandalas are spiritual arrangements of objects, usually circular in shape and visually striking. The fun of mandalas is that everyone can participate with well wishes and blessings for the guest of honor. Collaborative mandalas are often the most creative and unique with so many energies and intentions coming together as one.

Gather mandala supplies for your next birthday party, housewarming, wedding or baby shower celebration and let the sacred beauty unfold.

MATERIALS

- Flowers, leaves, crystals, etc… you can use any materials you wish! If you are stumped, look online for visual inspiration, there are so many beautiful earth based mandala artists. If you gather materials from the land, please leave an offering from your medicine bag in gratitude.

THE CEREMONY

1. Awaken sacred space before the mandala making begins.

2. As the ceremony leader, I often like to lay out some sort of initial framework of flowers, leaves or stones to help guide a basic shape within the space we are going to use. You can work on the earth, on a table or on the floor. You can place paper down if you want to keep your items contained or just work freely. The choice is yours.

3. Share the intention of celebration with your participants and explain a bit of the prayer process. I like to have everyone connect to a blessing for the guest of honor and then use the breath to infuse prayer into the mandala ingredients. Once infused, materials can be placed within the mandala. I often like to include a crystal that becomes charged with all of the mandala's blessings. When the natural materials are put back to the earth, the crystal can be gifted to the person you are celebrating as a keepsake of all the blessings!

4. Allow the creativity and intention to rise as the mandala comes together.
5. Once complete, close sacred space.
6. If you have worked indoors, at the end of the gathering, bring the natural materials outside as an offering to pachamama.

NOTES FOR YOUR OWN CEREMONY

HONORING THE SUN

Our relationship with the sun is essential! Inti Tayta or father sun provides our warmth, our light, and nourishment for our food. So many of my ceremonies are in honor of pachamama, whom I love dearly, but I wanted to also bring a reminder of gratitude to her counterpart!

During the winter, in certain locations, we can almost lose sight of the sun where his visits may be missing for days or even weeks! He will go into hiding much earlier in the day and come out to play much later. And then, we have the magical days of summer where the daylight seems to never end. All of the phases of our seasonal cycle help to shape our personal rhythms, our practices, and our traditions.

Honoring the Sun is a wonderful ceremony to perform on the solstices and equinoxes, recognizing the season that lies ahead and the solar cycle we are entering into. It may be that we are sharing our gratitude for the small sparkles of sunshine we receive in the winter or focusing on intentions of how we wish to use those extra hours of summer light. Whatever the time of year, we have ingrained seasonal practices that are completely connected to the sun's cycle. This ceremony is a way to bring awareness and gratitude to the sun's incredibly important role in our lives.

MATERIALS

- Offerings of flowers, leaves, stones, herbs, seeds, etc. whatever you wish!

THE CEREMONY

1. Awaken Sacred Space outdoors where you can connect with the spirit of the sun.

2. Spend a few moments in meditation feeling the sun's rays, warmth, and light to whatever degree is possible on your chosen day.

3. Create an offering of beauty with the materials you've gathered. If you gather the materials from the land, be sure to leave an offering from your medicine bag in thanks. Infuse each object with your gratitude prayer through your sacred breath. You can create a mandala, a sculpture, a cairn, you name it! Be creative and let your intention shine as brightly as the sun itself.

4. Close sacred space and leave your offering for the sun to watch over as he feels your loving prayers.

ALIGN TO THE DIVINE

No one is immune to those confusing, sticky, unclear circumstances in life that prevent us from charging forth. We all hit blocks at one time or another where we feel so disconnected that we can't even choose between turning left or right... saying yes or no... choosing chocolate or vanilla. Sometimes we need to stay put and await the truth to reveal itself. But other times, the answers are completely and immediately available to us if we can align ourselves with the clear whispers of spirit. The way I align myself to this knowledge base is through this very ceremony.

As someone who thrives off of creative work, I needed to find ways early on to connect to sources of divine inspiration and to bust through creative blocks. The work in my life that I am most proud of is not what has been manufactured by my mind. Instead, they are the works that have been inspired by journeys, meditations, and ceremonies where I have been given opportunities to converse with spirit.

Now, whenever I am stepping into the creative process, this is my go-to ceremony to fully align myself in order to create from a place of pure inspiration. I also use this exact same ceremony to find answers to life's trickiest questions. I have used it to write books, to help guide my location changes, to navigate business decisions, and to figure out how best to share my energy with others.

I find this ceremony to be incredibly effective at clearing away confusing mind chatter, sweeping out fear, and re-tuning your frequency so you can truly trust the answers you receive without question.

Like many ceremonies, this is a practice and the most profound results will come with some commitment to repeating this process. You may wish to begin with simple questions as you deepen your practice and save the juicier questions for when you have some experience under your belt.

MATERIALS

- A rattle or drum - I work best with a rattle, but the choice is yours. Try both if you can to find your best tool.
- Your medicine bag
- A journal & pen

THE CEREMONY

1. Awaken sacred space in a quiet location where you wish to work.

2. Call on your messengers! You may wish to call on a power animal, a force of nature, a particular spirit guide, your santa tierra (the spirit of your land), or whoever is your messenger of universal knowledge.

3. Make an offering to spirit from your medicine bag.

4. Sit or lay comfortably. Clearly state your question to spirit and set your intention to journey for this knowledge.

5. Begin to rattle or drum with a regular rhythm that is fairly quick and monotonous.

6. Place your complete focus on the rhythm. Feel it within your body and hear it in your ears. The rhythm will begin to pulse through your entire being. If you have trouble focusing, it is super helpful to tap your free hand (if you are rattling) or sway your body lightly with the same rhythm. You want this beat to completely overtake all that you are. It is here that your mind chatter turns off and that inspiration can come to life.

7. Stay here for a good 15-30 minutes. Try to avoid thinking about finding the answer in these sacred moments. Of course you want your intention to remain strong, but we aren't exactly searching for the answer… we are waiting for it to come to us. Oftentimes, the information comes to me later in the day or through journaling after this ceremony. Just keep your focus on the rhythm and this will work for you.

8. When you feel complete, put your rattle or drum down. Stay quiet for a minute and just observe. Notice how you feel, notice the thoughts that return and notice any bits of inspiration that are appearing. I always feel a little high at this point and find it a great time to pick up my journal and write down thoughts without censoring any of them.

9. Keep aware the rest of the day as messages appear in mysterious ways! This ceremony invites in synchronicity, so you may see your answers showing themselves in a completely unpredictable fashion. I received the message to sell my house when I "randomly" heard from 3 people within a single day that they had sold their homes and how free they were feeling. I wanted that same freedom and started my process (which went like a breeze with the divine timing!). This is the flow of synchronicity that I work to live in, always!

10. The more you keep up with this practice, the better the info you will receive. It really takes some experience to truly quiet your mind and sit with the rhythm for a good chunk of time, like any meditative practice. But it does get easier and more powerful as you progress. Having a tool like a rattle or drum is far easier than sitting silently and trying to achieve the same clarity (for me).

11. Close your sacred space when you are complete with gratitude for your messengers and the powerful answers they delivered.

> *I used this exact ceremony numerous times in the creation of Living Sacred Ceremony. There is no shortage of miraculous information you can gather when you intentionally tap into the wisdom of spirit.*

NOTES FOR YOUR OWN CEREMONY

STRENGTHENING FAMILY ROOTS

With the pace of our lives and the priorities of individual goals, it doesn't take long for our family connections to loosen. Add in the drama that absolutely no family is immune to, and we quickly realize that the health of our family bond does take some cultivation.

Can we begin to forgive? Can we start to build a bridge to healing our wounds, piece by piece? Can we return to the essence of family—unconditional love and support—and start anew? Sacred ceremony can be an extremely powerful way to deepen or rekindle our familial connections.

This ceremony can also be a sweet and beautiful way to bring two families together as one. For example, when single parents remarry into families with other children.

This practice is extremely simple, so bring your highest intentions and most refined focus to create powerful shifts!

MATERIALS

- A large bowl filled with water
- Flowers of choice, one or two for each participating member of your family

THE CEREMONY

1. Gather everyone in a circle with the bowl of water in the middle. Bring focus and intention with an opening prayer. You can follow the process for Awakening Sacred Space (page 15) or create a special prayer just for this ceremony. It can be very powerful for everyone to speak out their own intentions to reconnect or heal.

2. Have everyone use their breath to infuse their flowers with the intentions that they just shared, as well as any that they have chosen not to speak aloud.

3. Take turns, placing your flowers in the bowl of water, allowing them to float and mingle together as they infuse the water with your prayers.

4. After a few minutes of infusing the water, allow everyone to take a turn visiting the bowl again, this time taking some of the water and touching it to your belly, your heart and your third eye, at the center of your forehead. This is a process of receiving the collective prayers and allowing it to inform you on an energetic level.

5. Once complete, you can offer this time to share any experiences and then, close your sacred space. You may choose to keep the bowl of flowers on an altar or return them to the earth as an offering.

NOTES FOR YOUR OWN CEREMONY

FIRE CLEANSE

I believe that most of us are quite familiar with the idea of cleansing our bodies of toxic buildup in order to feel most vibrant in a physical sense. But what about the heavy residue that lives in your energy body (the energetic field that surrounds the physical body) from bad relationships, unhealthy work environments, unresolved conflicts, or other energetically toxic experiences? There's a cleanse for that, too!

In my life, I have found that spiritual hygiene can truly influence the health and vibrancy of the body. So just as we eat right and exercise, we want to remember techniques to keep our energy body clear and clean, strong and healthy. Our physical, emotional, and spiritual health are all linked at these roots.

To me, the element of fire is extremely quick and effective when it comes to energetic self-cleansing. Though I have many methods of helping others remove unwanted energies used within my healing practice, I often recommend fire ceremonies as follow-up and self-care. Fire burns off sticky energies and brings light to the darkest and heaviest of them all.

Use this ceremony to do a nice deep cleansing and then return to it as maintenance whenever you are feeling a bit off. This is the perfect ceremony for when you've had a confrontational encounter and want to shed the heaviness that remains.

MATERIALS

- A method to build a nice, safe fire outdoors. Follow proper fire safety techniques.
- Your medicine bag, a small despacho or another gift or offering to give to the fire. Let the beauty of your gift show your strong intention for healing.

THE CEREMONY

1. Awaken Sacred Space in the location you will use to build your fire.
2. Build and light your fire. Call on the spirit of fire to join you as you watch the flames grow strong.
3. Sit in prayer, in song, in intention. Choose your own way to honor the spirit of fire and speak your intention of cleansing and healing aloud.

4. Bring a gift to the fire as your offering. Use your breath to infuse the gift with a strong prayer of gratitude for the fire's healing powers. Place the gift in the fire and let it burn.

5. Once you feel that your gift has been accepted and it has burned completely, you may begin to work with the fire for your cleansing. Sit, stand, or kneel safely, close to the fire.

6. Use the energy of the fire to cleanse your energy body by waving your hands over the fire and then over your body. Carry the energy of the fire throughout this process with intention and prayer. Use common sense to do this intentionally without actually touching the flames.

7. Keep engaging in this process while focusing on any areas of your body/energy body that feel particularly heavy or sluggish.

8. To finish your process, bring the element of fire into your three main energy centers: your belly, heart and third eye. This will clean out any heavy energies and bring light to burn out the darkness that is stuck within.

9. Once complete, sit with the fire in quiet reflection while it finishes burning. Say a few words of gratitude to the spirit of the fire.

10. Close sacred space and make sure your fire is completely out before leaving it.

NOTES FOR YOUR OWN CEREMONY

BRINGING BALANCE

Life moves so quickly and for many of us, it seems like we are always leaning more in one direction or the other. We are either working too much or we can't find a job. We are on a super strict diet or we are completely letting loose. We are exercising all the time or we are stagnant. We have too much heat in our bodies or too much chill. We are sad or ecstatic. We live in extremes, but might it be possible to live in balance?

If I try to create balance too literally in my life, I find that every single time, I fail. Life has a way of ebbing and flowing. Sometimes I have the time and energy to do everything I want and sometimes I just don't. So, instead, I choose to look at balance in a metaphorical way. I incorporate the elements of earth, air, fire, and water. I look at my life as an ecosystem that needs to manage all of these powerful forces at once, in harmony. And sure enough, whether my schedule has changed or not doesn't really matter. Through ceremony, I feel better and I feel balanced.

All of the elements are reflected within us. If we are too deep into the earth, grounding is no question, but we may disconnect from our spiritual vision. If we live with too much lightness and air, we are spiritually linked but also may feel spacey and ungrounded. If we have too much raging fire, we may be super passionate, yet angry and reactive. If water is in excess, we may flow well, but might have trouble just stopping and committing to one thing. Building a ceremonial altar to these four elements in relation to how they are reflected within can be an important key to finding peace in the flow of our daily lives.

Imagine the peace and harmony of being both well grounded (earth) and spiritually connected (air). See yourself full of passion and fiery drive (fire) yet able to go with the flow and adapt when necessary (water). This is the intention we hold for this ceremony.

MATERIALS

- A rock or some other representation of earth
- A feather or some other representation of air
- A candle or some other representation of fire
- A vessel of water or some other representation of water
- A surface to build your altar, indoors or outdoors
- Fabric to cover your altar, if you desire
- Offerings from your medicine bag or any other lovely gifts you wish to bring to your altar

THE CEREMONY

1. Awaken sacred space in the location you have chosen to work. In your prayer, call on the spirit of earth, air/wind, fire, and water.

2. Prepare your altar space with a cloth if you chose to use one.

3. Pick up your earth object. Connect in with your relationship to earth in a quiet meditation. Do you have too much of this element? Too little? Just the right amount? What would you like the earth element to look like in your life? Speak your prayer to the spirit of the earth, to pachamama, and place the object on your altar.

4. Sit with the object representing air and wind. Connect in with your relationship to air in a quiet meditation. Do you have too much of this element? Too little? Just the right amount? What would you like the air element to look like in your life? Speak your prayer to the spirit of the wind and place the object on your altar.

5. Now visit with the object you have to represent fire. If it is a candle, light it. Connect in with your relationship to fire in a quiet meditation. Do you have too much of this element? Too little? Just the right amount? What would you like the fire element to look like in your life? Speak your prayer to the spirit of fire and place the candle on your altar.

6. Finally, sit with the object you have to represent water. Connect in with your relationship to water in a quiet meditation. Do you have too much of this element? Too little? Just the right amount? What would you like the water element to look like in your life? Speak your prayer to the spirit of water and place the object on your altar.

7. Now visit with the entire altar as one, in complete harmony and balance. Place your offerings to the spirits of earth, air, fire, and water on the altar in a way that connects them all as one powerful and harmonious energy.

8. Sense how peaceful this feels and try to embody this energy in any way that you can so you may carry it forth into your daily life.

A sense of balance is not a reflection of your external circumstances. It is an energy that you can tap into within yourself—no matter what is happening in your surroundings.

9. Close sacred space.

10. You may leave the altar set up to really enforce this work over time, returning regularly to make offerings. Or you may close the altar when you feel complete.

NOTES FOR YOUR OWN CEREMONY

CLOSING THOUGHTS

I truly hope you have enjoyed your ceremonial journey and that your results have been most profound! Remember, powerful ceremonies can be incredibly simple as long as your devotion is deep and your intention is strong. May this experience inspire the creation of your own unique ceremonies as well as a lifelong commitment to communing with spirit for your happiness and well-being.

I adore seeing your gorgeous offerings and hearing your ceremony success stories! Please share your photos on instagram with the hashtag **#livingsacredceremony** to spread the good word with our growing community of ceremonialists

ACKNOWLEDGMENTS

The foundation for my ceremonial work is based on the teachings of Jose Luis Herrera and his Andean Medicine Community through the work of ARI - Andean Research Institute. In particular, the Water Blessing, Despacho Ceremony, and Fire Ceremonies have been inspired by specific Andean teachings and ceremonies. Please visit www.andeaninstitute.org to see how you can be a part of their growing mission to support Andean and Amazon cultures by preserving medicine and textile traditions, women's empowerment, children's education, and land protection.

With love & blessings,

ABOUT NATALIA

I am a lover and practitioner of shamanism, herbalism, and sacred ceremony.

I have a BA in Studio Art and an incredible love to create. Though my medium has changed over the years, my passion for bringing beauty into the world has never diminished. Within my shamanic practice, it is the gorgeous prayer ceremonies that light me up so fully. Through herbalism, it is the alchemy of plants turned body-mind-soul medicine that enchants me.

I have trained extensively through The Four Winds Society, Jose Luis Herrera, and The Boston School of Herbal Studies. I have also been blessed enough to receive rites of passage and training from multiple medicine lineages—and from the land itself—in the high Andes of Peru. Shamanism and herbalism merge seamlessly as a deeply empowering path and I am incredibly grateful to live as a modern day medicine woman.

No matter what project I have my hands in, my intention is to always create from an earth-centered and spirit-guided space and to bring beauty, healing, and empowerment to the world.

I started my online shop, the Sweet & Sacred Botanica, as an expression of all that I am. It is the most complete representation of my soul, fusing artistry, shamanism, and herbalism—and the wonder contained in each. I take pride in creating healthy, organic, and ethically wildcrafted products for ceremony, healing, and beauty. And it is my greatest honor to share them with you.

Though I am a wanderer at heart, I am currently living and loving in Massachusetts with my web designer husband where we enjoy exploring nature, sitting in ceremony, laughing like crazy, and dreaming up our next adventure.

Learn more and keep up to date with my adventures at www.sweetandsacred.com.

Made in the USA
Middletown, DE
11 November 2016